TODAY'S SPORTS STARS

Bobby Witt Jr.
Baseball Star

FOCUS READERS
BEACON

by Anthony Streeter

www.focusreaders.com

Copyright © 2026 by Focus Readers®, Mendota Heights, MN 55120. All rights reserved. No part of this book may be reproduced or utilized in any form or by any means without written permission from the publisher.

Focus Readers is distributed by North Star Editions:
sales@northstareditions.com | 888-417-0195

Produced for Focus Readers by Red Line Editorial.

Photographs ©: Scott Winters/Icon Sportswire/AP Images, cover, 1; Ed Zurga/Getty Images Sport/ Getty Images, 4; Charlie Riedel/AP Images, 7, 29; Focus On Sport/Getty Images Sport/Getty Images, 8; Shutterstock Images, 11; Mike Janes/Four Seam Images/AP Images, 12; Zachary Lucy/ Four Seam Images/AP Images, 14; Dustin Bradford/Getty Images Sport/Getty Images, 17; Scott W. Grau/Icon Sportswire/AP Images, 19; Harrison Barden/Colorado Rockies/Getty Images Sport/Getty Images, 20; Quinn Harris/Getty Images Sport/Getty Images, 23; Brandon Sloter/Image Of Sport/ Getty Images Sport/Getty Images, 25; Red Line Editorial, 27

Library of Congress Cataloging-in-Publication Data
Library of Congress Cataloging-in-Publication Data is available on the Library of Congress website.

ISBN
979-8-88998-597-6 (hardcover)
979-8-88998-623-2 (paperback)
979-8-88998-614-0 (ebook pdf)
979-8-88998-606-5 (hosted ebook)

Printed in the United States of America
Mankato, MN
082025

About the Author

Anthony Streeter is a former sportswriter and avid golfer from Columbia, Missouri.

Table of Contents

CHAPTER 1

Rounding the Bases 5

CHAPTER 2

Baseball Family 9

CHAPTER 3

Climbing the Ranks 15

CHAPTER 4

King of the Royals 21

At-a-Glance Map • 26

Focus Questions • 28

Glossary • 30

To Learn More • 31

Index • 32

CHAPTER 1

Rounding the Bases

The pitch sped toward home plate. Bobby Witt Jr. took a huge swing. He sent a line drive into the outfield. The Kansas City Royals' star sprinted to first base. Then something unexpected happened.

The Kansas City Royals played the Seattle Mariners on August 14, 2023.

5

The Seattle Mariners' right fielder lost the ball in the stadium's lights. It bounced past him and toward the wall. So, Witt kept running. He rounded first base. Then he headed past second. Finally, the center fielder reached the ball. But Witt

Did You Know?

Witt rounded the bases in only 14.3 seconds. That was baseball's fastest inside-the-park home run in six years.

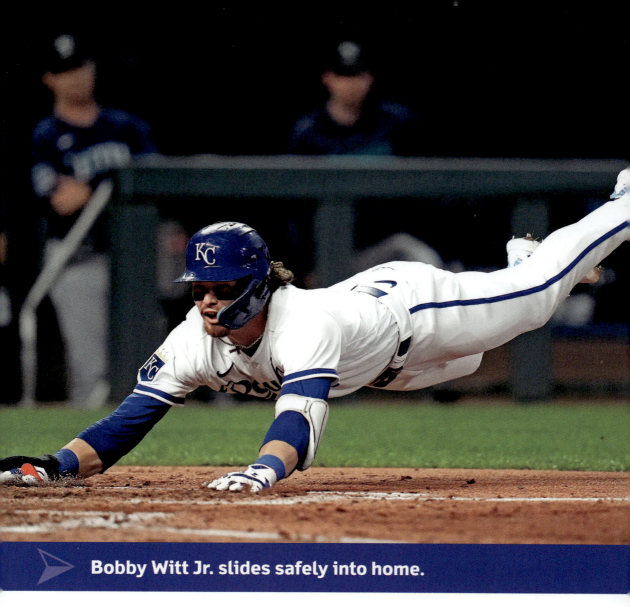

Bobby Witt Jr. slides safely into home.

was already turning toward home. He slid headfirst over the plate. It was an inside-the-park home run!

CHAPTER 2

Baseball Family

Bobby Witt Jr. was born on June 14, 2000. Everyone called him "Junior." His dad, Bobby Sr., was a pitcher in the major leagues. Bobby Sr.'s career was almost over by the time Junior was born.

Bobby Witt Sr. played in the majors from 1986 to 2001.

The Witts lived in Colleyville, Texas. After Bobby Sr. **retired** from the majors, he had lots of time to play with Junior. Bobby Sr. passed on his love of baseball. And he helped Junior improve quickly.

At age seven, Junior started going to a local baseball camp. Everyone knew of his dad. Soon, they knew about Junior, too. Other kids were amazed by his quick swing.

Junior's talent was clear. But he kept working hard and getting

Colleyville is a few miles away from Dallas, Texas (pictured).

even better. As a **freshman**, he became the starting shortstop for Colleyville Heritage High School.

Junior was a **mature** player. He could stay calm in big moments.

11

Bobby Witt Jr. hit a three-run homer in the 2018 Under Armour All-America Game.

He always kept his focus. He was athletic, too. Junior made big hits and diving catches look easy.

Scouts ranked Junior as the best high school player in the United States. So, he decided not to go to college. Instead, he went straight to the pros. The Kansas City Royals had the second pick in the 2019 Major League Baseball (MLB) **Draft**. The Royals selected Junior.

Did You Know?

Five days after the MLB Draft, Junior led Colleyville Heritage to its first state championship.

CHAPTER 3

Climbing the Ranks

The Royals believed that Bobby Witt Jr. could be a star. But even top baseball **prospects** start in the **minor leagues**. In 2019, Witt played in a league for first-year players.

 Bobby Witt Jr. played in 37 games in 2019. He piled up 43 hits during that time.

Witt quickly got used to the tougher competition. He was already a great hitter and a fast runner. He was a versatile fielder, too. Coaches thought he could play just about any position in the majors.

Witt was excited for 2020. But the season never happened. COVID-19 spread around the world that spring. Minor league baseball was canceled for the year. Instead, Witt spent the summer training.

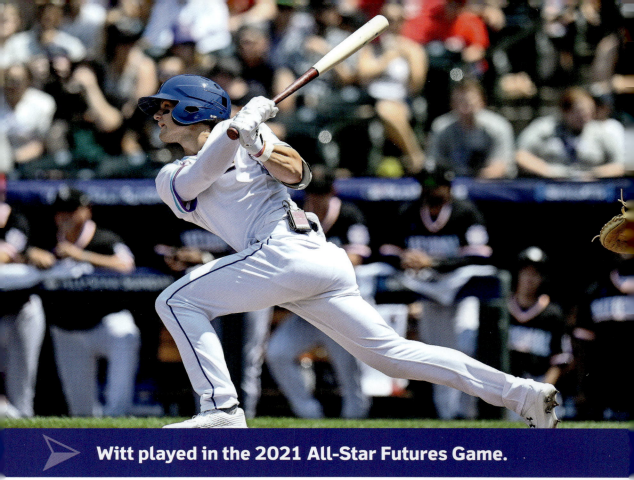

Witt played in the 2021 All-Star Futures Game.

The young star still got a chance to impress his coaches in practices. They had high hopes for him in 2021. He moved up to Double A. That is two levels below the majors.

Witt was ready for the higher level. As a fielder, few balls got past him. He also had a strong arm. Hitters struggled to reach bases before Witt threw them out. By the end of the year, he had moved up to Triple A.

Witt excelled in Triple A, too. He made good decisions at the plate.

Did You Know?

In 2021, Witt hit 17 homers during his time with the Royals' Triple A team.

Witt often used his speed in the minors. He recorded 29 steals during the 2021 season.

He showed off his powerful swing. By 2022, he was ready for the next step. Witt made the Royals' Opening Day roster. His MLB career was about to take off.

CHAPTER 4

King of the Royals

Right away, Bobby Witt Jr. showed off his talents at the plate. In his first MLB season, he recorded 150 hits. That included 20 home runs. However, Witt made lots of mistakes as a fielder that year.

 Bobby Witt Jr. stole 30 bases during the 2022 season.

So, he worked hard to improve. He practiced his timing and **reflexes**.

By the next year, Witt was one of the best fielders in the league. However, his 2023 season got off to a slow start as a hitter. That changed in late July. The Royals faced the Minnesota Twins. The game was tied in extra innings. Witt stepped to the plate with the bases loaded. Then, he crushed a fastball into the stands for a grand slam. The play showed Witt's incredible

In 2023, Witt helped turn 69 double plays.

bat speed. It also kick-started his season.

The Royals ended 2023 without many wins. Even so, Witt showed his leadership skills. Other players fed off his hard work.

The next season, Witt improved even more. In 2024, Witt earned his first batting title. He was also clocked as baseball's fastest player. He even won a Gold Glove for his **defense**.

The team saw more success, too. Witt's strong play lifted the Royals

Did You Know?

Witt made his first All-Star Game in 2024. It was held just a few miles from his hometown in Texas.

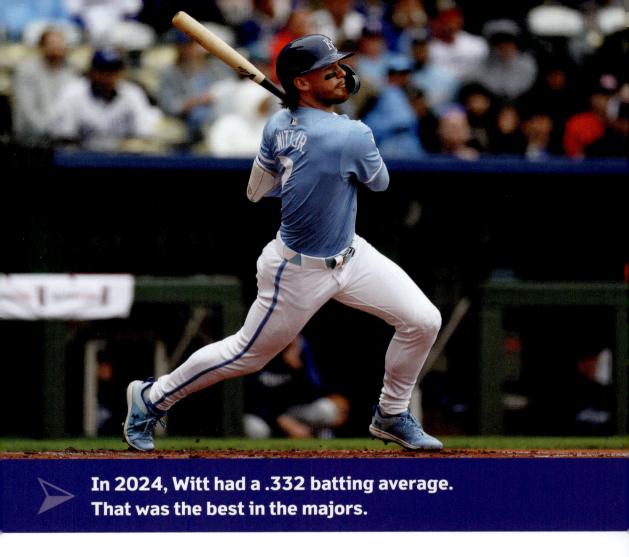

In 2024, Witt had a .332 batting average. That was the best in the majors.

into the postseason for the first time in nine years. With Witt at shortstop, the future once again looked bright in Kansas City.

AT-A-GLANCE MAP

Bobby Witt Jr.

- Height: 6 feet, 1 inch (185 cm)
- Weight: 200 pounds (91 kg)
- Birth date: June 14, 2000
- Birthplace: Colleyville, Texas
- Minor league teams: Arizona League Royals (2019), Northwest Arkansas Naturals (2021), Omaha Storm Chasers (2021)
- MLB team: Kansas City Royals (2022–)
- Major awards: MLB All-Star (2024), Gold Glove (2024), Silver Slugger (2024)

Focus Questions

Write your answers on a separate piece of paper.

1. Write a few sentences explaining the main ideas of Chapter 3.

2. What do you think Bobby Witt Jr.'s most impressive skill is? Why?

3. Against which team did Witt hit an inside-the-park home run in 2023?
   - **A.** Minnesota Twins
   - **B.** Texas Rangers
   - **C.** Seattle Mariners

4. How many minor league teams did Witt play on?
   - **A.** two
   - **B.** three
   - **C.** four

5. What does **versatile** mean in this book?

*He was a **versatile** fielder, too. Coaches thought he could play just about any position in the majors.*

    A. not able to learn or change
    B. able to do only one thing
    C. able to do many different things

6. What does **excelled** mean in this book?

*Witt **excelled** in Triple A, too. He made good decisions at the plate. He showed off his powerful swing.*

    A. performed well
    B. decided something
    C. struggled

Answer key on page 32.

29

Glossary

defense
The skills involved with stopping the other team from scoring.

draft
A system that allows teams to acquire new players coming into a league.

freshman
A first-year student.

mature
Acting grown-up or like an adult.

minor leagues
The lower levels of a sport.

prospects
Players who are likely to be successful in the future.

reflexes
Quick responses or movements.

retired
Ended one's career.

scouts
People whose jobs involve looking for talented young players.

To Learn More

BOOKS

Anderson, Josh. *Kansas City Royals*. The Child's World, 2024.

Hanlon, Luke. *Kansas City Royals All-Time Greats*. Press Box Books, 2024.

Tischler, Joe. *Kansas City Royals*. Creative Education, 2024.

NOTE TO EDUCATORS

Visit **www.focusreaders.com** to find lesson plans, activities, links, and other resources related to this title.

Index

A

All-Star Game, 24

C

Colleyville, Texas, 10
Colleyville Heritage High
    School, 11, 13

D

Double A, 17
draft, 13

G

Gold Glove, 24
grand slam, 22

I

inside-the-park home
    run, 6–7

M

Minnesota Twins, 22

O

Opening Day, 19

S

Seattle Mariners, 6

T

Triple A, 18

W

Witt, Bobby Sr., 9–10

Answer Key: 1. Answers will vary. 2. Answers will vary. 3. C. 4. B. 5. C. 6. A